The Holy or the Broken Hallelujah

poems by

Kristina Hakanson

Finishing Line Press
Georgetown, Kentucky

The Holy or the Broken Hallelujah

Copyright © 2022 by Kristina Hakanson
ISBN 978-1-64662-757-8 First Edition
All rights reserved under International and Pan-American Copyright Conventions. No part of this book may be reproduced in any manner whatsoever without written permission from the publisher, except in the case of brief quotations embodied in critical articles and reviews.

ACKNOWLEDGMENTS

"The Harrow" appeared in *Reunion: The Dallas Review*, 2020
"Loyalty" is forthcoming in *Without a Doubt*, an anthology of poems about faith, published by New York Quarterly 2022

Several poems have appeared, in slightly different incarnations, in my blog www.logic0fwings.wordpress.com

Many thanks to my teachers and the MFA program at Pacific University, especially Joe Millar, Ellen Bass, Steve Kuusisto, and Marvin Bell; and to the fellow writers who provided critique and inspiration along the way: Paulann Petersen, Elaine Nussbaum, Karen Holman, Gwen McNeir, Kari Wergeland, Dawn Robinson, and Helen Gearhardt. And to my husband, Jonathan Brechner, sincere love and gratitude for the whole journey.

Publisher: Leah Huete de Maines
Editor: Christen Kincaid
Cover Art: Kristina Hakanson
Author Photo: Kristina Hakanson
Cover Design: Elizabeth Maines McCleavy

Order online: www.finishinglinepress.com
also available on amazon.com

Author inquiries and mail orders:
Finishing Line Press
PO Box 1626
Georgetown, Kentucky 40324
USA

Table of Contents

Being Here Now 1
Childhood 3
Eggbeater and Wooden Spoon 4
Stars 5
Equinox 6
Late Anthropocene 7
Yogi 8
Rocky Point 10
Moonlight 11
Iron 12
The End of Days 13
The World Is Not What We Thought It Was 14
Loyalty 15
The Wolf in the Cello 16
Heaven's Underside 17
Empties 18
The Holy or the Broken Hallelujah 19
Utopias 20
Eve as Bodhisattva 21
Out of Square 22
Ebb 23
Suite of Grief 24
Absolutes 28
The House/Body Hieroglyph 29
The Harrow 30
In Speaking to the Dead 31

Being Here Now
Remembering Ram Dass (1931-2019)

I'm in a coffee shop killing time while my son grits his teeth
at Club Tattoo a couple of blocks down & his inky
blueblack rose blooms itself into being above his heart

(bewitching connotation isn't it, to blossom, to be in flower),
for how do we become anything except by becoming it?
Try to remember being almost nineteen

with its timeclocks & guitars & half-understood term papers
not so alien a life as that of the great horned owl
hoo-hoo-hooo-ing from the arroyo this morning, maybe

saying goodnight. My perfect cappuccino is soon gone
while the cataract so small & the tinnitus bearable
& the probably-benign tumor in the right breast just is.

Twelve days of Christmas dwindle to their partridge,
finally, the year nearly pissed entirely away.
The best I can do is count the minutes until cocktail hour

monkey-minding on blind ole Milton
deaf ole Beethoven & too many womenfriends
all self-aware when their organs & glands gave them notice

& they, composed, composed—oh, but how
did they forgive their aberrating bodies?
Not new *to*, but bad *at* inventing our rites of passage.

Confident of the flowers that wink at paradise,
soothed by the piano sonata & with luck
we think we decide for ourselves from which shore

to disembark, good at improving our selves
& practicing careers & religions. But maybe
we misread the directions: is it *into* adulthood or *out of* teens?

through middle age & decline or *beyond* the hormonal embers?
On which elevator is it safe to ride up to enlightenment,
now that the whole place is in flames?

Childhood

Water in a green bowl,
swirling, dribbling, going, gone.

We live in liquids,
we believe in the water of memory.

I believe in milk with sugar and blueberries,
and in grandmother's silverware

rattling in the velvet green box,
and in the wisdom of old spoons

hand-washed, whispering concave secrets:
she is not beautiful but handsome.

He loves her cooking.
The two of them grow impossibly old,

but their hearts are not weak, yet.
The kitchen's black rotary-dial phone rarely rings.

Eggbeater and Wooden Spoon

I love the mechanical eggbeater
steampunk gearwheel
for whisking years
and wire cages shaped like light bulbs
except no ideas appear
as they did in '70s cartoons

and wooden spoons:
worn to inert peach fuzz
that causes shivers, even today,
cleaning up after making stew
I hear *I'm gonna paddle your behind
with a wooden spoon*

I must have been five at the time
and this the only terror
persisting in my fingertips
at the touch of wooden spoons
as if, in the mind's rotary beater,
I have never left that room

Stars

You are unbalanced by stars,
by their beckoning, like an ideal lover—
glittering, unattainable.
You will never touch them, though longing
briefly takes over on ordinary drives like this—
how cold you feel, how free,
how alone and capable—
why are you here?
Whole lives are lived on the dirt
which long ago came from the stars.
Your elements have always been theirs.
Someday you will give it all back to them,
unspooling light from beneath your ribcage
and let it go on, to wherever it goes.

Equinox

The summer dawdles even as it dwindles.
Just like me, losing calcium from my hipbones,
still wearing thong panties. The aging body
and ambition never quite make sense,
they merely go on. What hells we carry—
nightmares like murky photographs: blurred legs running
to a place we can't see.
                          Detach from your thoughts,
the wise tell me. Chop-chop, time's always wasting
and the dirt underfoot always ready to take us back.
So I pretend not to notice a lover's bad mood. I eat
the last bite of cake without regret.
Sunsets are beginning to work their way into my life
exactly the way sunrises did a lifetime ago
when I watched them alone, thinking.
                               Always thinking,
instead of licking the chocolate frosting from the plate,
always thinking, instead of holding hands in bed.
The hours, my god, creep at such a petty pace.
What's there to do but to rehearse falling in love?

Late Anthropocene

In this America, people plant both feet
in some hungry endeavor:
one foot in a watershed of hope,
one foot in the body's desire for oblivion.
You ransack the kitchen for nerve tonic.
Resist the impulse to pass judgement on yourself—
don't we all seek an anodyne for this life? After all,
you can almost reach the medicine shelf inside your soul.
If you do, gently touch maidenhair ferns,
the humble toadstools, the crickets, the wrens,
and all classes of shy mammals who live there.
Stand on the tips of your toes, very close to reaching
or knocking the whole thing down.

Yogi

I do not seek comfort from the bottom of the well
but I can't help knowing its dark, even pressure.
I do not seek the place where the echoes stop
and the waterdrop peeling from the bucket edge

finds its source in the old Rocky Point homestead font
which is both a mnemonic and a physical wellspring,
a seedbed, an origin, and a cradle.
I was six that summer and the well

was just boards over a deep hole,
wild grasses around,
brown Ponderosa needles, shimmering Aspens.
We kids would lower the aluminum bucket

with rope and bring cold water back up,
pretend this was daily life longer ago that it actually was
for my father and his mother and father.
I couldn't see the bottom, though I tried, the way I tried

seeing inside the pointy toe of a cowboy boot
forever the wrong angles and too dim.
Mystery and death were companions.
So when my father accidentally ran over

my brother's dog, Yogi, in front of us,
all these years later I remember dappled light,
diesel, squeal. My brother's arms waving
wildly. Diesel exhaust.

Blood on the dust tracks.
My father's wide blue eyes,
his confused face grown horrified at what he'd done
without knowing and never spoke of after that day.

Like the well.
What it would be like to rest in its fathomless end.

Rocky Point

I didn't know anything
except rhythms:
Dad's breathing,
Opa on all fours hammering
particleboard, bambamBAM,
the tape measure's tongue
returning itself to the metal case
in the delicious seconds
of blood rushing to the ears
of space heading backward
without taking time along
into the void where

at Rocky Point
my father and his father
tried to build a house
though fifty years
and a job and a family
separated them.
I was five when I thought I saw blisters
on my father's freckled back,
and worried until my mother said
only sweat

Moonlight

The June you are seventeen is warm and the moon is full. You drive 30-some miles, park, and pull off your t-shirt and Levi's, revealing a metallic, royal blue bikini—better than blue in the moonlight because it shimmers like your grandmother's platinum hair. The lake is still cold but the air is quiet and delicious, heavy with dust and pine, and you wade in, wobbling a little on the rocks. Sucking in breath, you push off with your toes, small waves lap like Velux blankets on your arms and you roll to your back and float and float. You stop when you're ready to stop.

There's the forest, dark and calm. There's the moonlit shore, bright and ready for you to come back. And here you are, alone in water, fully aware that the moon concatenates the soft animal of your muscles and breathing with this lake, this night, this dust and pine, this road leading here and now.

Iron

You are seventeen, the age when the mind begins its concessions to pleasure. Your boyfriend works in a butcher shop. Quitting time comes but the smell of the trade cannot forget him: trout and blood and cold streams in June—the kind of scent that only washes off partway. At its crudest and most dazzling, the body is meat, gristle, and bone. The body knows so much: iron and oxidation and the barefoot child's summer flirtation with wayward rusty nails and the threat of lockjaw. Flesh is the only thing on the mind. An hour after dusk, you sit on his mother's couch and he slides his hand under your shirt, knowing its way as simply as a skilled knife knows what it is carving. His brown hair smells red; yours holds onto dissipating coconut shampoo. Think about stars and skin cells, how they connect by light-years and dust. You remember watching grandmother clamp an ancient meat grinder to her kitchen counter; you see her hand on the crank, turning.

The End of Days
after Anne Waldman

There are no rats.
Hazmat labels peel apart
from their plastic bags.
Women are nauseated
and weepy, men give vacant stares.
No one finds the right words anymore,
as though it were ever easy
to find the right words.
Once, there were meadows
holding wildflowers.
The sun shone brilliantly.
Small insects pressed
their feet into petals, so many feet.
Now, meadows die. Ancient pollens,
mute and blind but not dumb,
wait for the other side to flip,
for what originates next—
what rain might instigate or wash away.

The World Is Not What We Thought It Was

1
At three a.m. daylight and a cheerful thought
are an unfathomable distance away. When we were young,
when we thought there was time to recover from our mistakes,
this waking never happened.
                                    The ordinary is the medicine:
check the cat's water dish, putter in the kitchen, read the news
and wait for light. Watch the birds at their feeders:
greedy flitting staccato: left, right, never satisfied.

2
An old dream haunts me: I am a ghost.
My mother, in her blue quilted robe, walks through me,
Stops at the kitchen table of my childhood
Where my father and brother are already sipping coffee
The three of them, like before I was born.
Whether life comes or goes, it always makes a circle.
They are solid. I am vapor.

3
In the mountains (the lungs and heart of the world),
our own dark waking is flipped as though God wields a spatula.
There's no time here, just rhythm—waking, walking, dreaming—
nothing much disturbs one foot in front of the other.
We respect the storm clouds
and the old snow on the riverbank.
Trusting deep, our own designs melt into water.

Loyalty

When I try to think of an exciting thing I own, I come up empty.
Pencil, fuzzy slippers, & of course the coffee cup,
beige ceramic, stackable
utilitarian & sturdy
the least exciting object in my possession
& how I enjoy it simply for its dull exactitude.
It does its job no more no less
like Cordelia's same devotion that so enraged Lear.
That's the other thing I love—
why should things be more in themselves than they are?
I remember my grandfather's ordinary mug
passed down to my father
& the unspoken respect
for dull possessions
that they expressed by using them correctly
by touching a smooth surface gently
washing it deftly, perfectly
& putting the mug in its rightful place
on a shelf alone yet with others of its kind.
Just as I have learned
to respect that which turns up silently:
the sunrise no matter how gray
the syllable the word the phrase
the bitter coffee and the buttery bread
a Saturday with no demands.

The Wolf in the Cello

A wolf can sometimes live inside a cello. I already know about pumpkin ale and brilliant, October sunlight filtering down to nightfall and a small circle of loved ones settling into an easy dinner. How lucky we are, to be here together and imperfect, with our reading glasses and stray hairs and pizza-splotched tee-shirts. My brother takes the new rent-to-own cello from its case and we all tune in to the tuning-up, the bow searching topographically for the skips—the wolf—wanting to be let out. This wolf doesn't howl, but it yelps a little across the strings, chased by the bow, pursued in a kind of persistence hunt. This wolf is not tired. This wolf doesn't leave its thin, wood-veneer home. How like the wolf I am, wanting to be recognized. How like the cello I am, defenseless in the skilled hands of a musician who tries to release a voice from the strings it was born with. How like the hands I am, rope-veined and sure of themselves, diagnosing the instrument, capably finding their way to the beginning of song.

Heaven's Underside

There ought to be an underside of heaven
just in case the topside isn't all it's cracked up to be.
Imagine it: ageing waitresses
with lacquered beehive hairdos become angels.
They call you "hon" and refill your cup, endlessly.
Imagine harp music gone out of fashion, so there are coffeehouses,
local microbreweries. Acoustic guitars,
saxophones, maybe a piano (you always liked the piano).
Who needs eternal life—plain old eternity is bad enough.
Things should end, and in this underside of heaven,
the bartender gives a last call on time,
the divorce papers are filed at the courthouse,
children grow up and have mediocre jobs,
which they're mostly grateful for.
Your sister's ashes stay cold in the urn.
Hearts and minds break and break and then mend
to your astonishment and relief,
like a country doctor suturing with silk thread
and whiskey. Each sorrow converted to ice
grows warm in the palm of your hand.

Empties

When I was twelve
my father gave me
a .22 rifle
and all I killed
were empty beer bottles
perched on weathered fence posts
like skinny brown men
awaiting their doom.
Sometimes,
when the pain
of waking up
is too much,
I can hear the firing
in all cells of my body—
splintering
then gone.

The Holy or the Broken Hallelujah

I keep thinking how we almost made it.
I keep thinking how spring is the season for resurrection:
how tall the grass is this year, striving,
juxtaposed with peeled paint and eroded plaster.
Undeniably, a structure still stands.
Hell, the roof looks mostly intact.
When she left, nothing decayed past a certain point—
artfully distressed like a photograph but not actually dead.
I can't bear demolition, rubble heaps, dust.
I prefer to give attention to the sunlight
covering the particleboard siding like veneer.
I believe in weedy possibility, the long *o* in home.

Utopias
    for Jonathan

In the utopia of costumes,
I try on my dead grandmother's wig.
Not her best one, but her house one—
acrylic, not human, hair—
and find solace when it doesn't fit.
In the utopia of skyscapes,
monsoon season. Creosote and rain.
I try to stay awake all night and watch lightning,
but electricity lulls me to sleep.
I wake up happier than I've been in a long time.
In the utopia of smells,
you place a handful of lavender flowers in my palm—
finally, a pungent reward
for crushing something
without anger. Once,
in the utopia of night,
we fell asleep holding hands, woke
still holding, morning songs echoing
from the hills, sky flooded with tremors,
in the utopia of birds.

Eve as Bodhisattva

She runs out of the blazing orchard, wearing only a tank top and shorts. You can't believe her skin—one hand will certainly be scarred and useless for life, but her face is miraculously fine. Dirty though—like in movies. Tear-streaked. At first she doesn't speak so you try asking her questions: What's your name, where does it hurt? Some trees were meant to burn, she says. You wake up, sweating, calling out the names of skydivers, engineers, artists, each name endowing the dream with something more than smoke. You want this woman to have more, she deserves more help than you can give her at four a.m., even as you try erasing the smell of seared flesh from your mind. You want her to know she woke you up—that you will try to stay awake as long as you can. You want her to have one of your past lovers, one who still lives in your dreams, someone who will minister to her, someone who can fly.

Out of Square

While my father recuperated from urostomy surgery,
he kept his hands busy at a fabric loom,
a softer pursuit than his usual cordwood runs
(he did all the cutting and loading himself)
or building birdhouses,
or raised garden beds, re-purposing
old park-bench planks & never calling it "re-purposing"
because to his way of thinking
one simply finds a use for a good, straight plank.
Those winter months
he took up fabric-weaving
& made a striped rug,
the least likely thing he ever made.
He got the tension right,
he got a good variety of spring green, mustard yellow,
& tomato red—Mom helped him there.
He wasn't proud of it:
Two of four straight edges.
Never would he tolerate a thing out of square.
But I wanted something that he made
with his own hands,
wanted again, like the times
when I was small
& he made new plywood-and-wire hutches
& nesting boxes for my rabbits
all of which had perfect right angles,
so I got the rug. He got used to new plumbing
& a new resignation to imperfections,
humbled by the body that failed
& by the part of himself that accepted it.

Ebb

I'm too late for this party.
My mother in her blue quilted robe
does not make me feel guilty.
She leaves long before I do, smiling.
Half-deflated helium balloons
wander on air currents
like silent but happy guests.
This is the house
I wish I had appreciated
when I was twenty-five.
Half-eaten cake,
vanilla frosting stuck to the floral china,
twisted blue crepe paper streamers,
duckie pins,
all of it a merry riot
that I used to know.
This is not tragedy.
This is the blithe ebb
of time
with its fading carnations,
its sunny and empty rooms.

Suite of Grief

The Hospice Meeting

Them
in my father's hospital room
me
at my desk a thousand miles away
us
in disbelief

Parataxis

seeing my father
thinner than believable
knowing his time in this present world is short, shorter
than is bearable. He's ready to go—
lingering is not his style

ideas
      ideas
           abstractions

abstractions—death, dying
all abstractions
like a trance
until I hear my father's pragmatic
I suppose your mother will sell the house.
Thank you for taking Johnny's pistol.

PHX to MFR

Gratitude for the Bob Ross t-shirt
because people smile & say I remember
him on TV & they say awesome shirt

thus removing me from the grief inside
so a shirt walks around gate C17
with me inside it
where the magma-core pain lives.
I'm about to say goodbye
to my bedridden father, the first man I loved,
the only one whose heart I refuse to break,
ashamed that I ever did,
if I ever did.
I'm sure I did.

Haze

Haze from the fires in California and Oregon.
Mountains barely visible in the basin.
A buck nibbles his way through the back field, Boris meows.
This is as normal as it can be, for now,
but I've been in my parent's bedroom,
perched on the neat-as-a-pin bed
that neither of them use now.
He's still asleep in his hospital bed in the living room
and she's across the room on the sofa.
They're both sleeping in—already 6:30.
The sky is a version of rose gold,
the late-summer landscape mostly yellow.
Mom let the lawn die, too much to take care of
and Dad her priority. Haze closes us
in its weird blanket, telling us this is how the weather is changing,
coming between us and the blue sky,
even though we're still grateful for any light at all.

The sun is a red inferno in the east;
Always this time of year, oppression literally hangs in the air.
But this is not a regular fire season—

it came early and might linger another month—
so his last summer does not blaze,
it smolders and spits and coughs,
it lies still and stiller.
Maybe hope exists because we believe in the earth's
turning and turning. The gifts of night and day
are still here, geese fly in Vs.
I just wish fire season would end.

Grieving His Body

the bone bone bone
the never-to-heal sores
red heels
twin stomas and plastic bag hookups
teeth so long, receding gums
lips that stick to tissue as I wipe them gently
thin skin (not a metaphor)
rigid cold toes cold elbows
purple and clammy hands
eternally unbreathing chest

Bottomless

there's no bottom to grief, no stopping the tree's fall down to the center of the earth

in mourning the soul performs its many dissertations upon the soul

if Time is an apple corer, I am hollowed, only intellectually believing in Time's green spring, someday he belongs to the past now—and the deepest present, the internalized now, fully oxygenated red blood cells circulating, the atoms of carbon, the protein strands of my hair, the refrain measure twice, cut once

"...we thought we was gettin' away with somethin'" he said, about borrowing Neal's big brother's motorcycle without permission, back in high school; they taught themselves to lean into the road's curves, no helmet, never fell

Absolutes

Never the same, never to recover, really, from this loss. Always carrying his love of morning light, the scent of pine, the laughter of small children. Always the finality of waxy skin. Always the fact of being in the room when he exhaled for the last time, or Jon carrying his body to the gurney at the top of the stairs. Always my cowardice, reticence about shaving him (the CNA did it instead). Never telling him that I recorded him while we were talking a month ago, storying his past. Forever glad I recorded him before his voice faded to whisper. Always at odds: plans and time, days and filling them. Always nights and sweet oblivion. And a new absolute: always waking, seeing him in his hospital bed that hospice set up in the livingroom, the frailty I never believed in before now.

The House/Body Hieroglyph

In an unfamiliar house/body, alone, again,
& the bathroom is carpeted a graybrown Berber
& I may have to pee because why else would I be dreaming of bathrooms?
But I don't stay there
I explore the tiny hallway
& its cherry bookshelves full of pulp crime novels
that I will never read. But there is a pistol
& I'm overjoyed to find it.
I pick it up, spin the barrel, discover
it's only a toy. That's the moment I know
this dream is about my father.
My father's body becoming alien to him
forcing him to adapt after
his cancer
& his radiation
his urostomy
his colostomy
& his chemo
his compromised ability to mend
his endless vomiting
& not knowing his way around this: his body
failing for the final time.
The gun crossed his mind, too.

The Harrow

"America really is the story not of finding one's place but of leaving it."
        —Poe Ballentine

You're only leaving until you've left.
Before going, you hold up two mirrors
so you can watch your face contemplate future and past.
Leaving the old country, leaving jobs, leaving families, leaving life.
Then everybody is an American, no?
Like my first-generation father, and before that his immigrant parents.
And life is supposed to be for the living—
the upright, the breathing, the ones standing in line
at Starbucks, indecisive, not really thirsty, just killing time.
I found out that my father was mortal
when he couldn't recuperate from another surgery
and I remembered he used to say
"time and patience, patience and time"
for healing a sprained ankle, losing a boyfriend,
or anything that needed mending.
Just knowing he can't say it anymore
means I've left my country of origin.

One month after he died,
I woke without re-living his death
or seeing his thin, dead body,
feeling his cold elbows and arms,
witnessing his eyes which stayed open until the end.
I woke to a green, still meadow.
Maybe he finally saw the harrow he dreamed of the week before he died,
saw the ground massaged by the metal spines,
caught a whiff of manure,
felt the tractor's sure machinations and rumble,
knew and welcomed the knowledge of the ground.

In Speaking to the Dead

1
in speaking to the dead,
you do not open your mouth
no need to say the obvious
thus wax-grey mottled skin
says merely *time*

but that was weeks ago
in speaking to the dead today
the underside of heaven promises
to give you keepsakes
in the honest reality of ashes

like a membrane dividing two worlds
distinct from each other
permeable only in dreams
and only when you squint your ears
yet this pious Earth rotates

2
paycheck to paycheck the days churn
how do we make relevant
the working class lives
the aspirations upward—
my god can you ever stop the hissing in your ears?

chimes, singing bowls
castanets, cash registers
all ringing as the peak of Maslow's pyramid
stays within sight of our mind's dollar-bill-green eye
and there's a morning now

coming in on filaments of shadow
ghost robes, shrouds

the after-effects of a bad night's sleep
dreams by the side of the bed
with the hubcaps gone

Kristina Hakanson is a writer and English teacher who dabbles in photography. She hails from Klamath Falls, Oregon, and has had various careers in marketing, non-profit early literacy, communications, copywriting, and teaching, all of which were made possible by the unfairly mocked and utterly useful BA in English which she holds from the University of Oregon.

A graduate of Pacific University's MFA in Writing program with a concentration in poetry, Ms. Hakanson and her husband, fellow Pacific MFA alum Jonathan Brechner, wrote and independently published a collection of collaborative poetry, *The Ordinary Glow of Life*, and have a second collaborative collection in progress.

Recent poems of Ms. Hakanson's have appeared in *Basin Bards: Poems by 44 Klamath Poets, Reunion: The Dallas Review, ellipsis…, NonBinary Review, Broad Street,* and *Tinderbox*. She and her husband live in Arizona. logic0fwings.wordpress.com

Printed in the USA
CPSIA information can be obtained
at www.ICGtesting.com
LVHW041631280524
781601LV00003B/566